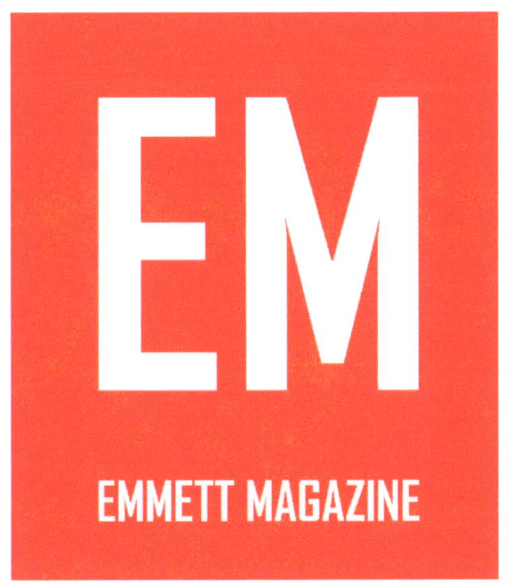

KATHERINE B. FOX

A MODEL & NURSE INTERVIEWS

PAGES 2-11

ALI RIZVI

STUDIO PHOTOGRAPHY

PAGES 2-5

ADAM JOY

COVER PHOTO & MILAN RUNWAY PHOTOGRAPHY

PAGES 9-12

CLAUDIO PARENTELA

MODERN ARTIST

PAGES 19-28

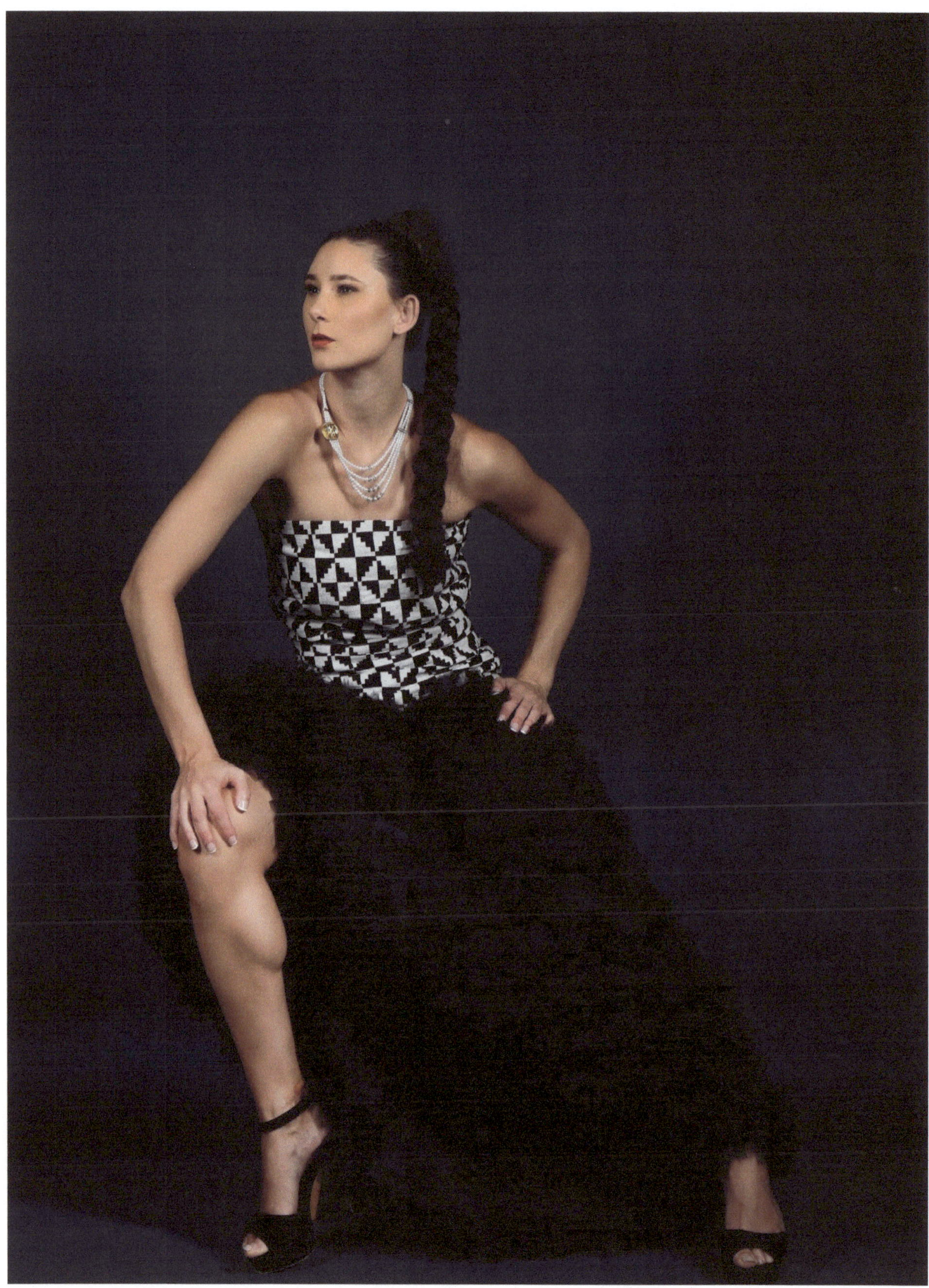

STUDIO PHOTOGRAPHY: ALI RIZVI **MODEL:** KATHERINE B. FOX **DESIGNER:** CLYOPATRA COUTURE **MAKE UP:** CHYNA LEWIS

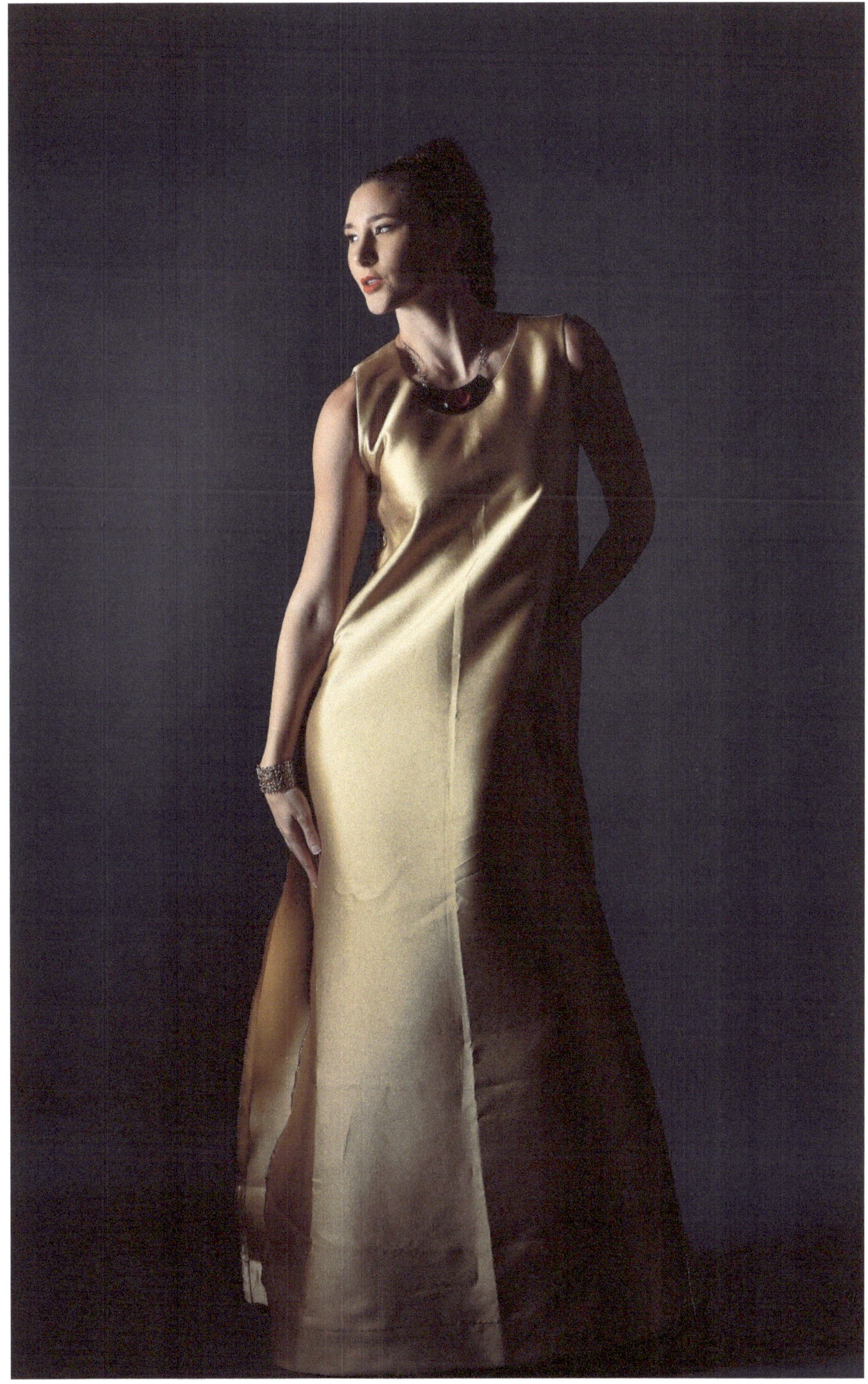

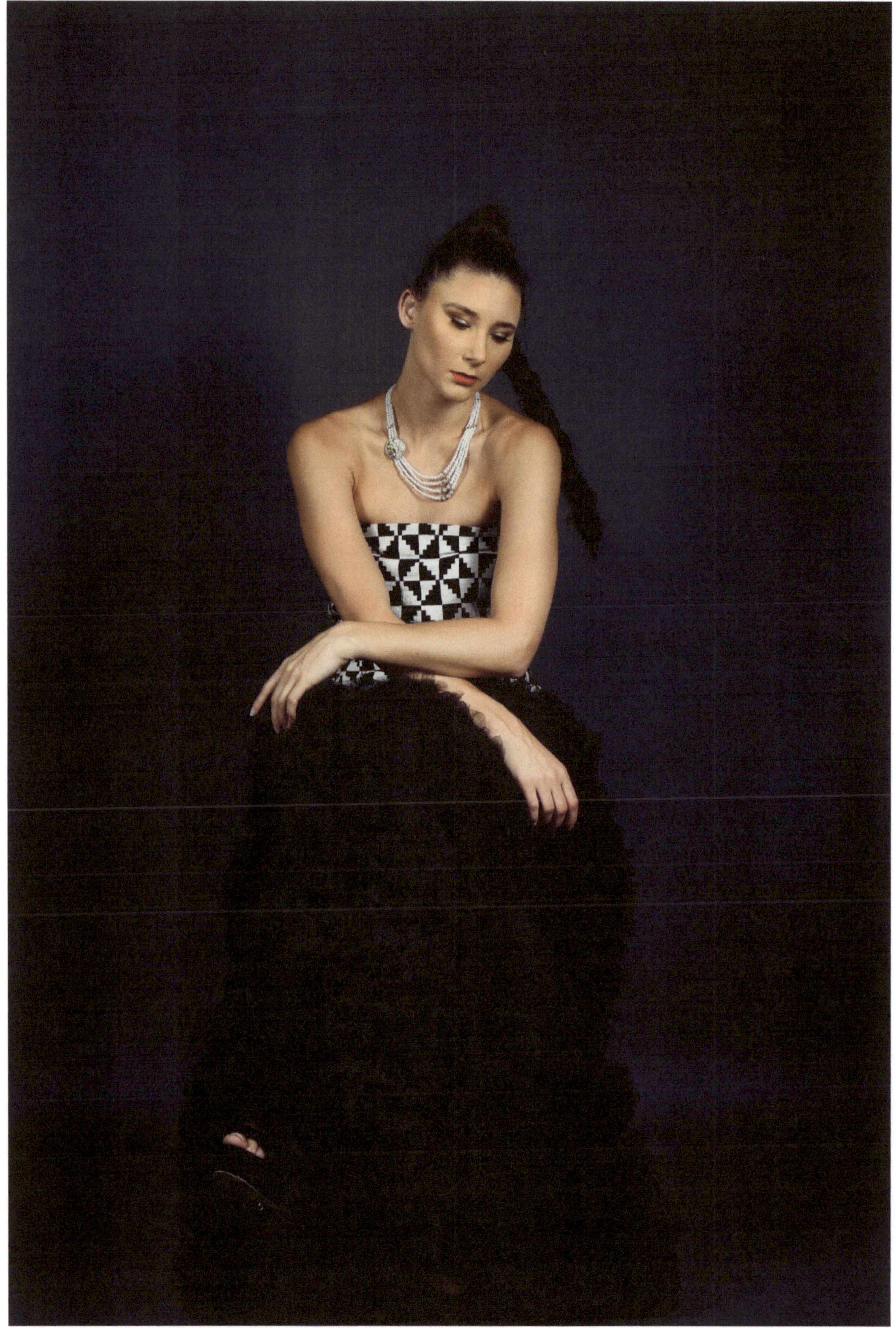

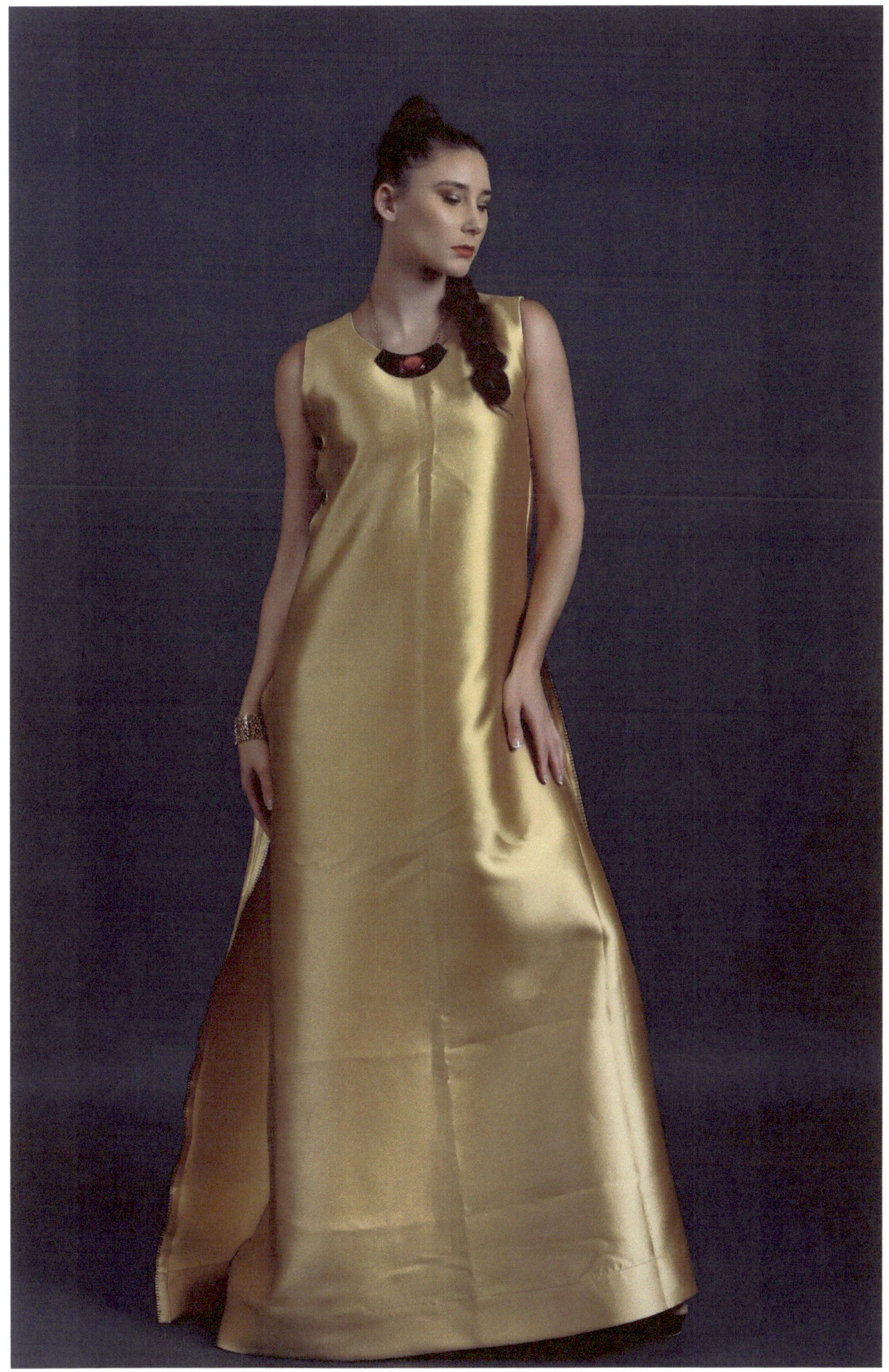

EMMETT MAGAZINE

INTERVIEWS

KATHERINE B. FOX

Where are you from and, what inspired you to become a model as well as a nurse?

I am originally from Khabarovsk, Russia, but was adopted and grew up in America. Nursing was my second degree. It's a Masters. I went back to school because I missed science and people, I previously had a desk job. After I became a nurse though, I got burnt-out and took a spur of the moment vacation by myself to Jamaica. I met a modeling agency there and we took photos all week long, I knew nothing about modeling, but loved it and got back to the states and started modeling along with my nurse job. I still work as a nurse and model now, but do travel nursing, so I can see the country and have new interesting places for model shoots.

Were there any early role models or mentors you can name?

Valentina Tereshkova. She was the first woman to fly in space, an engineer, and a member of the State Duma. A very inspirational figure!

Have you achieved all your ambitions in life…if not what's left on your bucket list?

I've achieved many of my bucket list items- go on a hot air balloon ride, have my research published in a medical journal, go to a rodeo, etc., but I still have a few to achieve like getting published in Vogue/Harper's Bazaar, fly first class, and buy a house along the water someday.

In the Modern Times we live in, technological advancements have enabled us to achieve the impossible with little or no time constraints Man was once burdened by. If you could achieve anything in the next 5 minutes…for yourself, family or the world what would it be?

It might take more than 5 minutes. Better healthcare. Better for the people who go through it, and better for the people who work in it. I would also achieve a healthcare system focused on preventative health. Active. Rather than reactive. As a cardiac nurse, heart disease is the leading cause of death in the United States, costing the US about $240 billion a year, with someone having a myocardial infarct every 40 seconds. It's often too late. And yet, much of this could be avoided with building an infrastructure focused on giving society healthier food options that are affordable and more opportunities to get out and be active. I would prioritize work/life balance.

Sources:

https://professional.heart.org/en/science-news/heart-disease-and-stroke-statistics-2022-update

National Center for Health Statistics. Multiple Cause of Death 2018– 2021 on CDC WONDER Database.

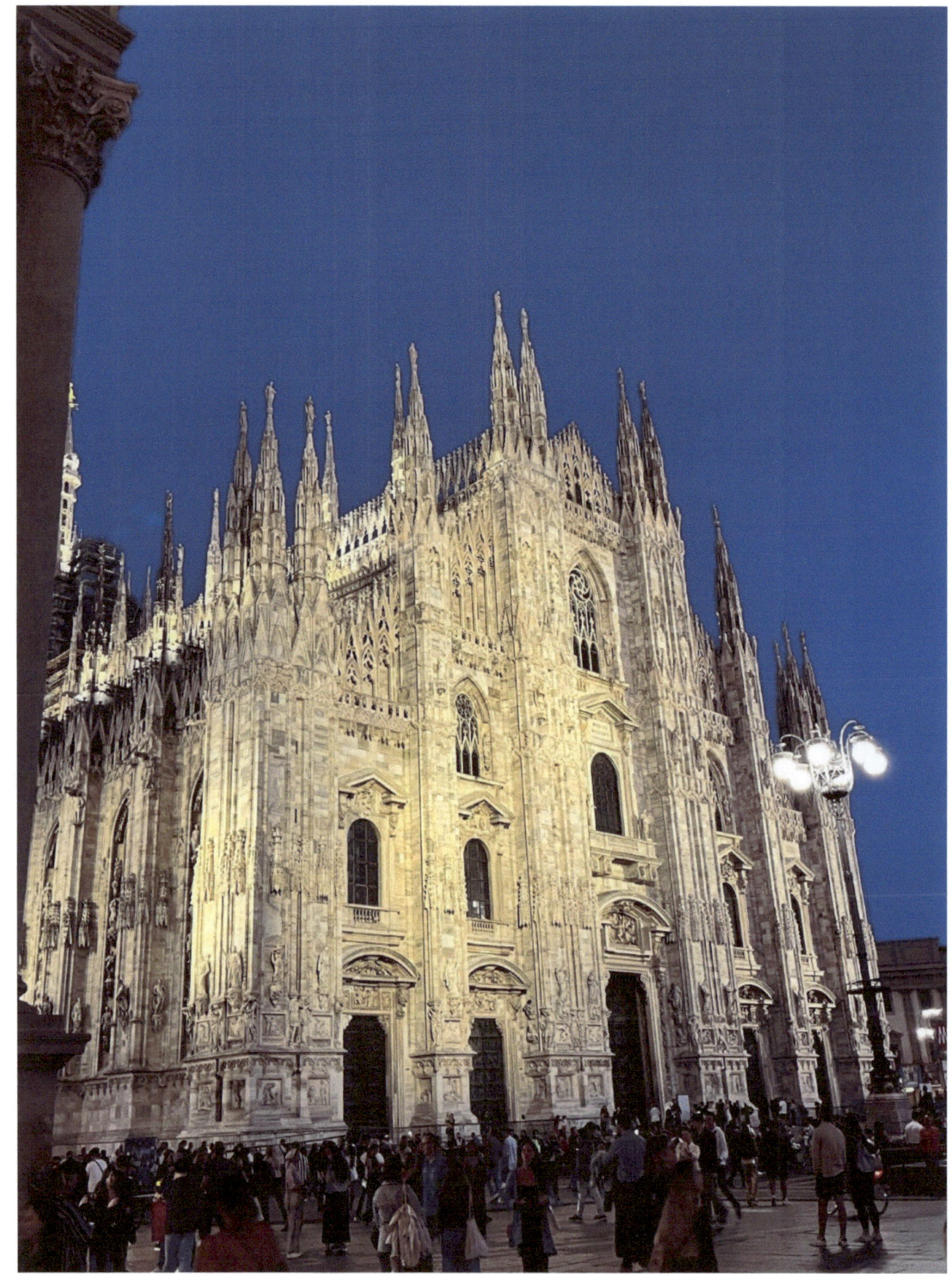

MILAN

THE FASHION LIFE TOUR

PHOTOS: ADAM JOY   MODEL: KATHERINE B. FOX   HAIR: BRENDA ACERO   MAKE UP: CLAUDIA TREJO

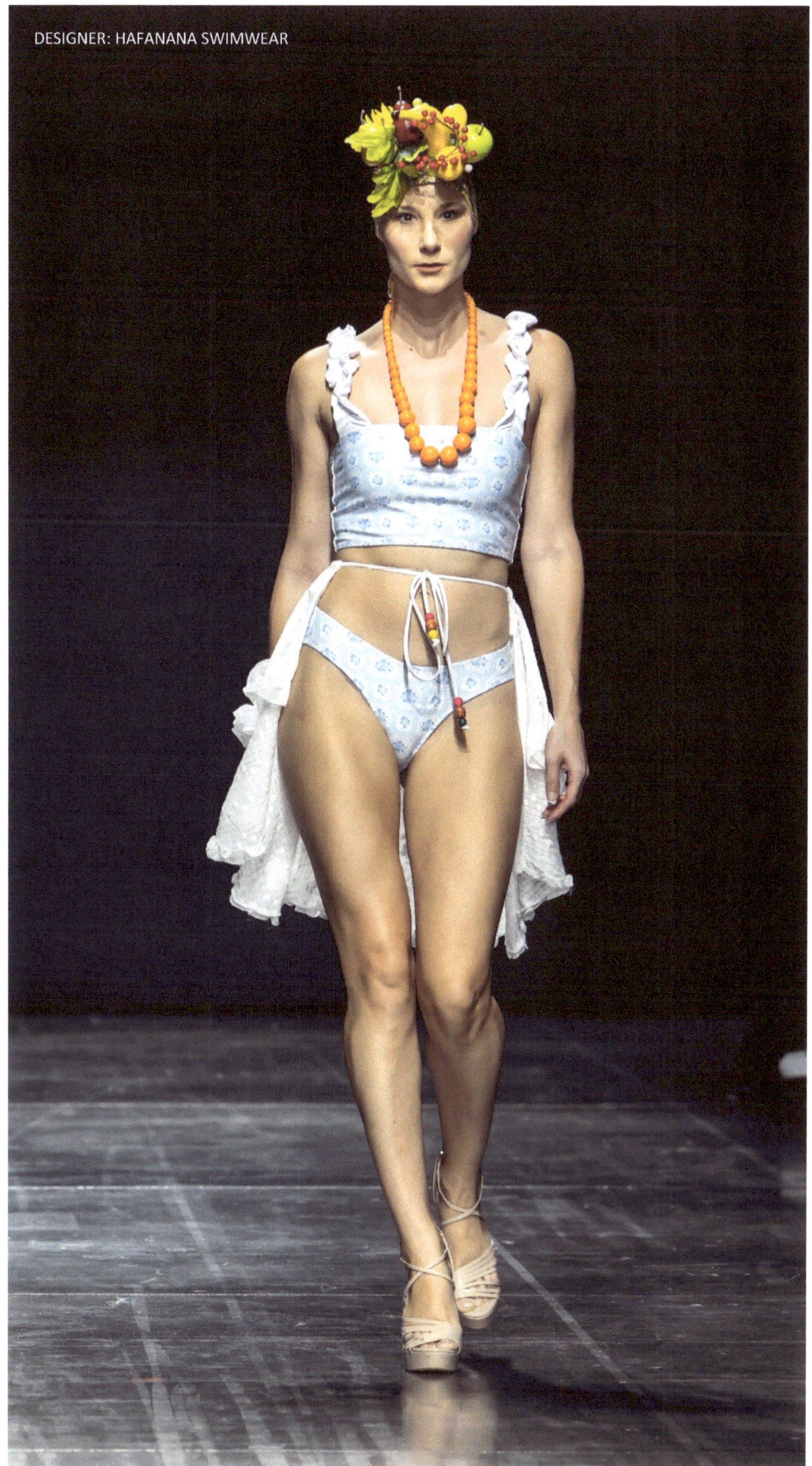
DESIGNER: HAFANANA SWIMWEAR

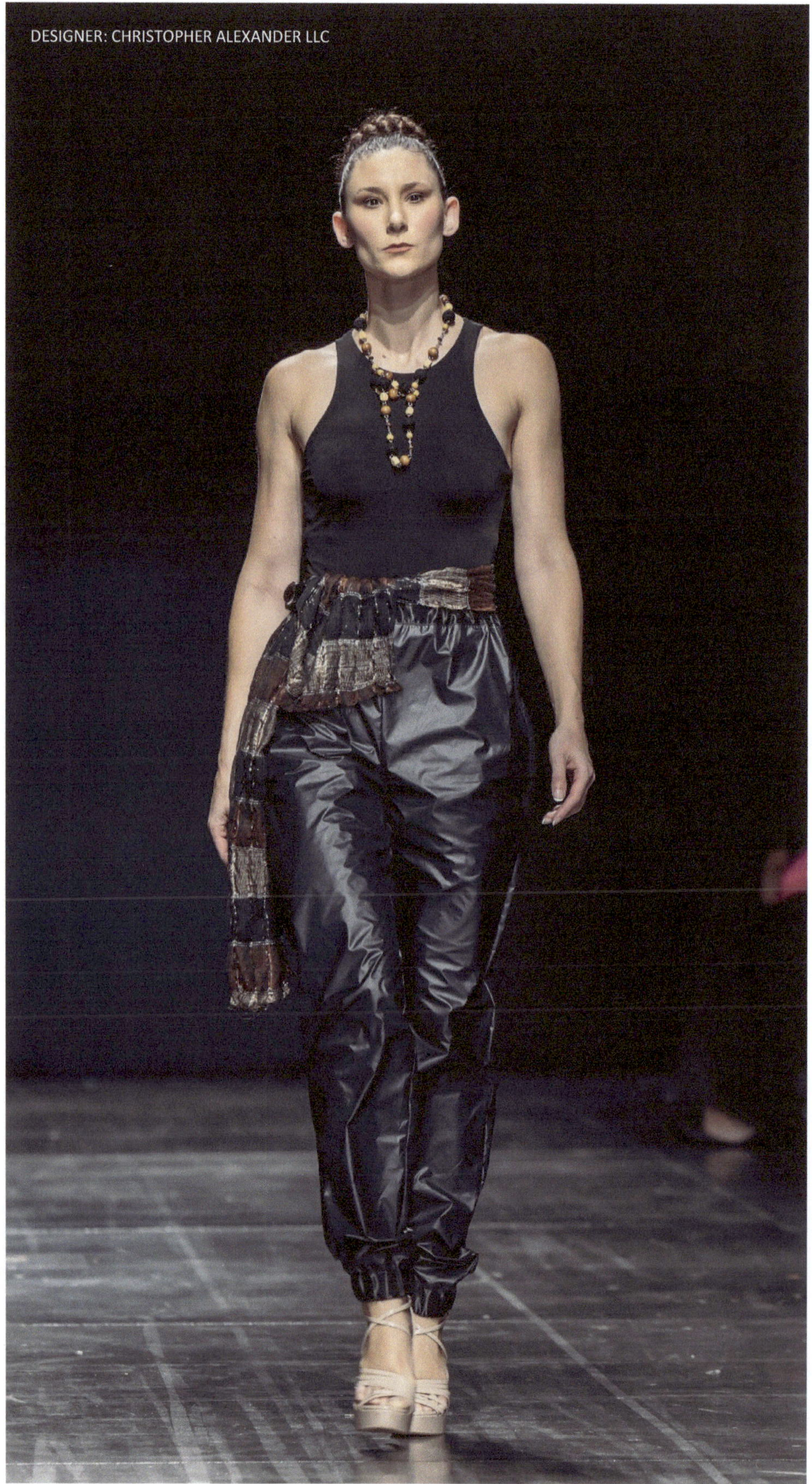
DESIGNER: CHRISTOPHER ALEXANDER LLC

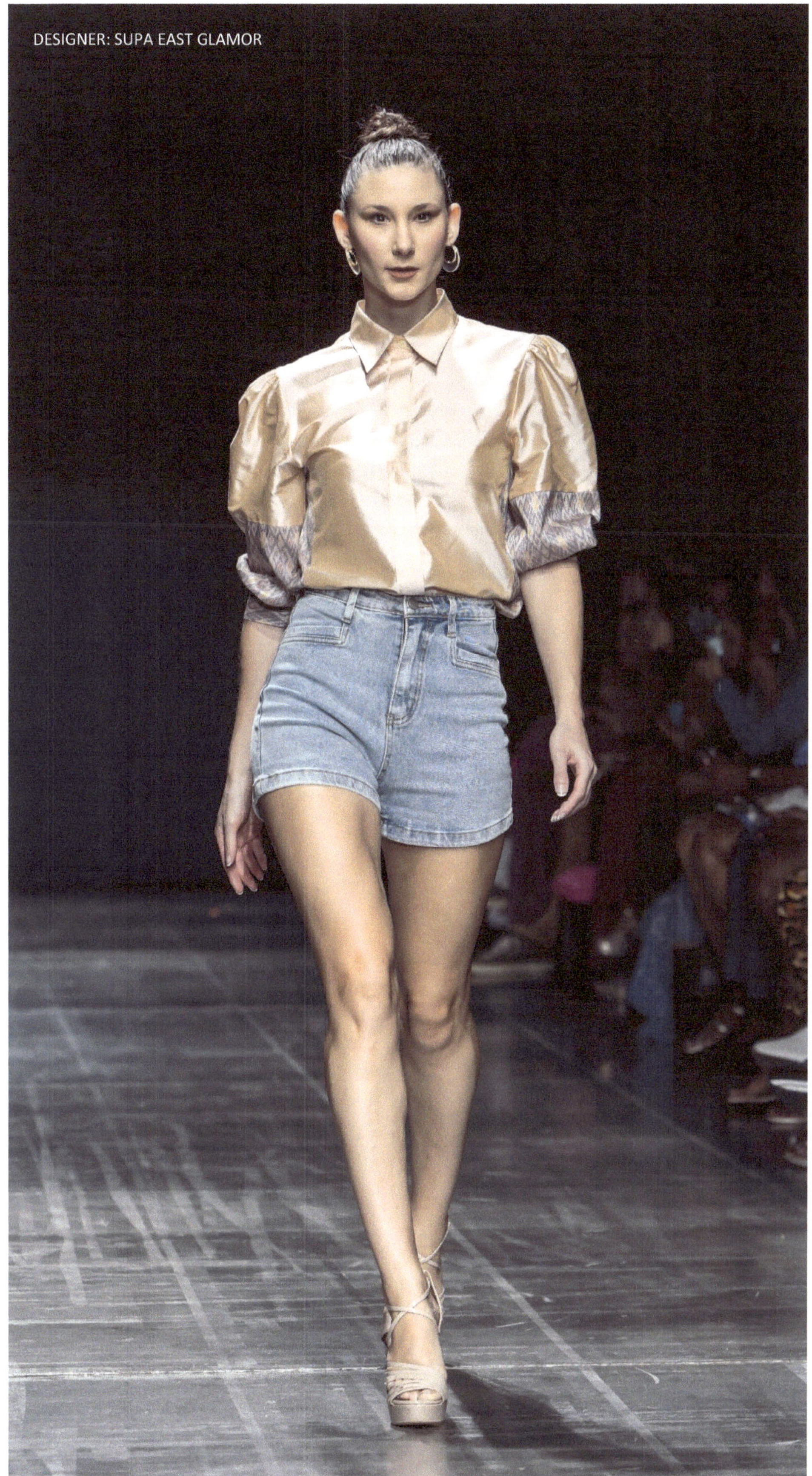
DESIGNER: SUPA EAST GLAMOR

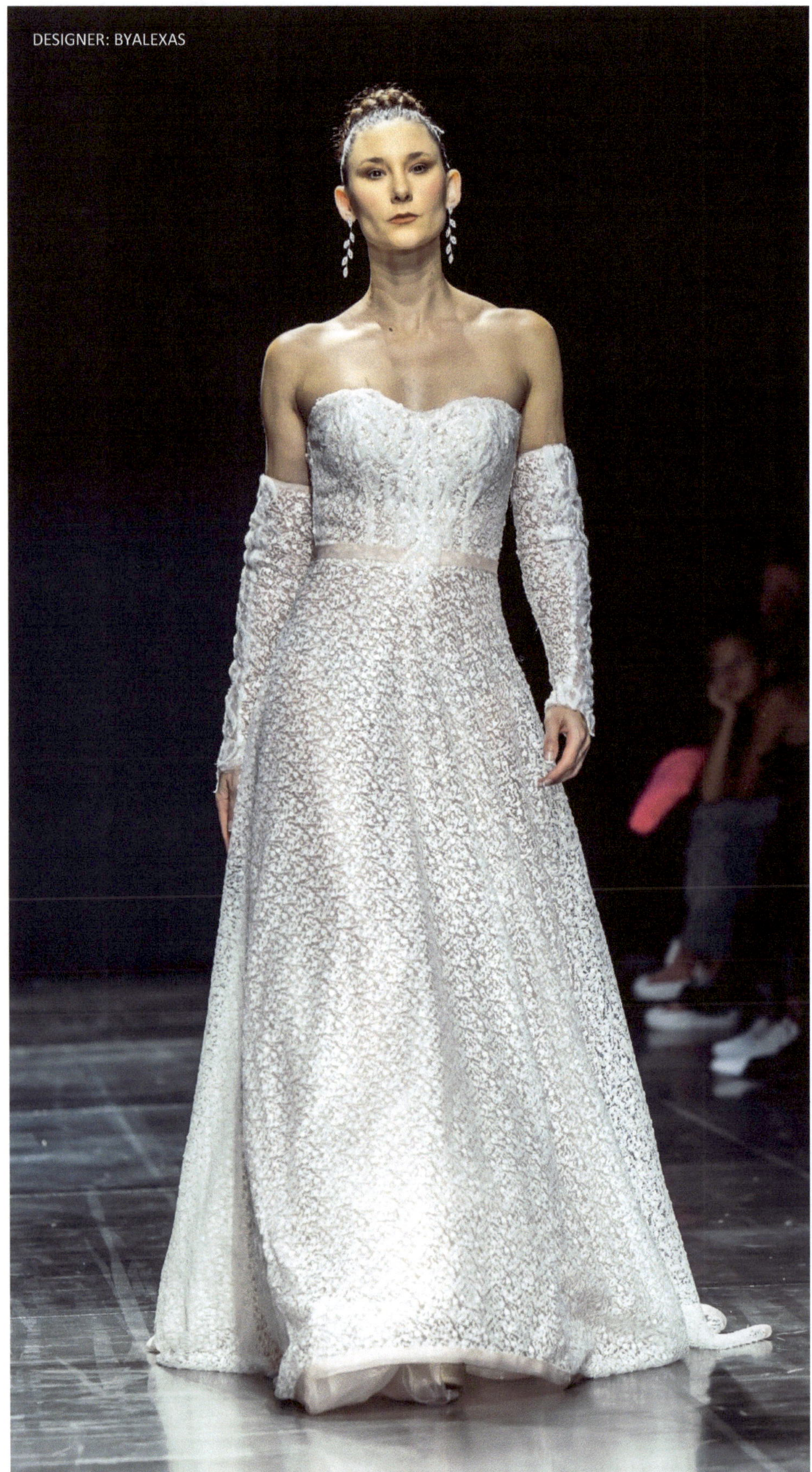
DESIGNER: BYALEXAS

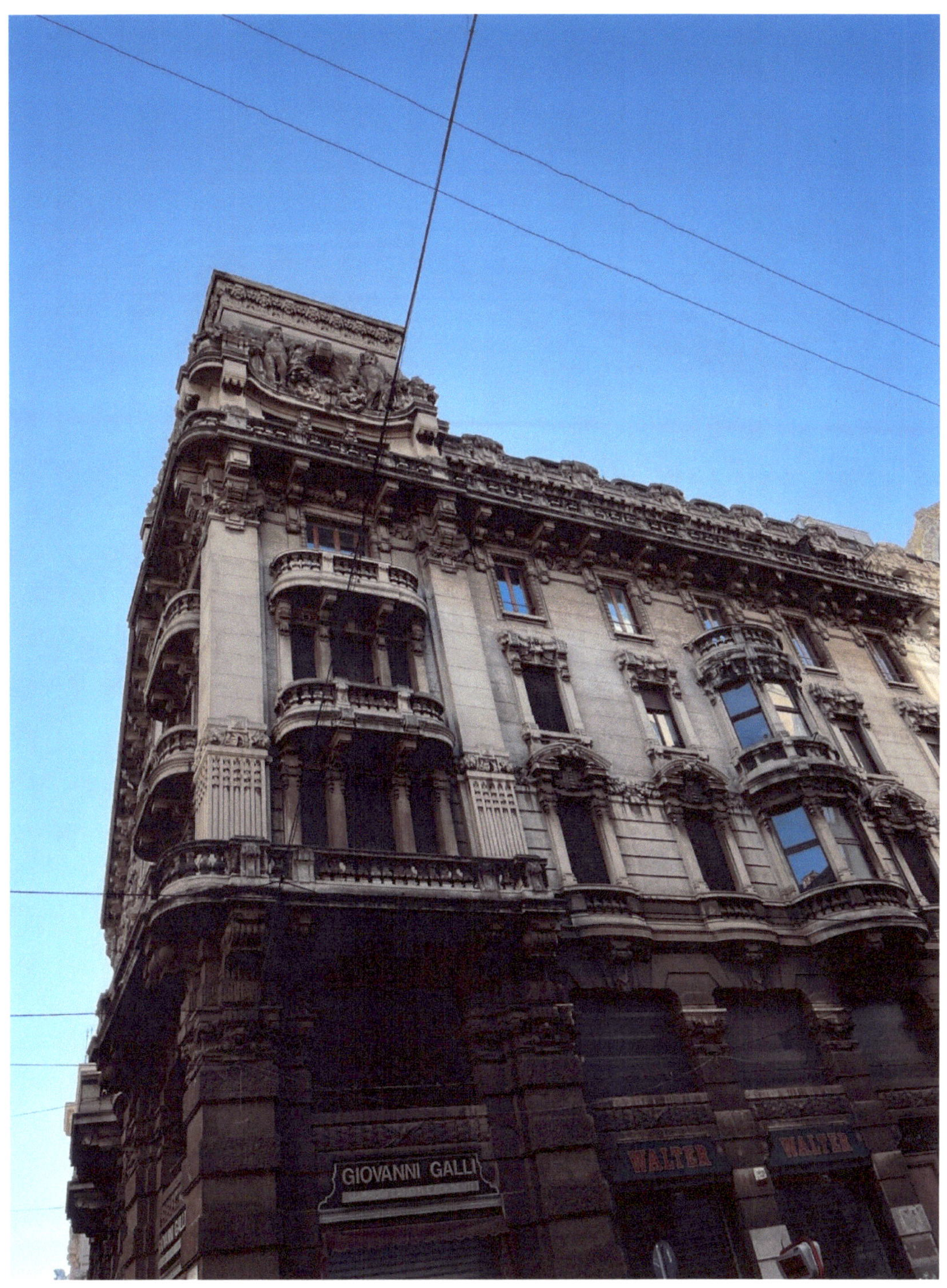
GIOVANNI GALLI
WALTER
WALTER

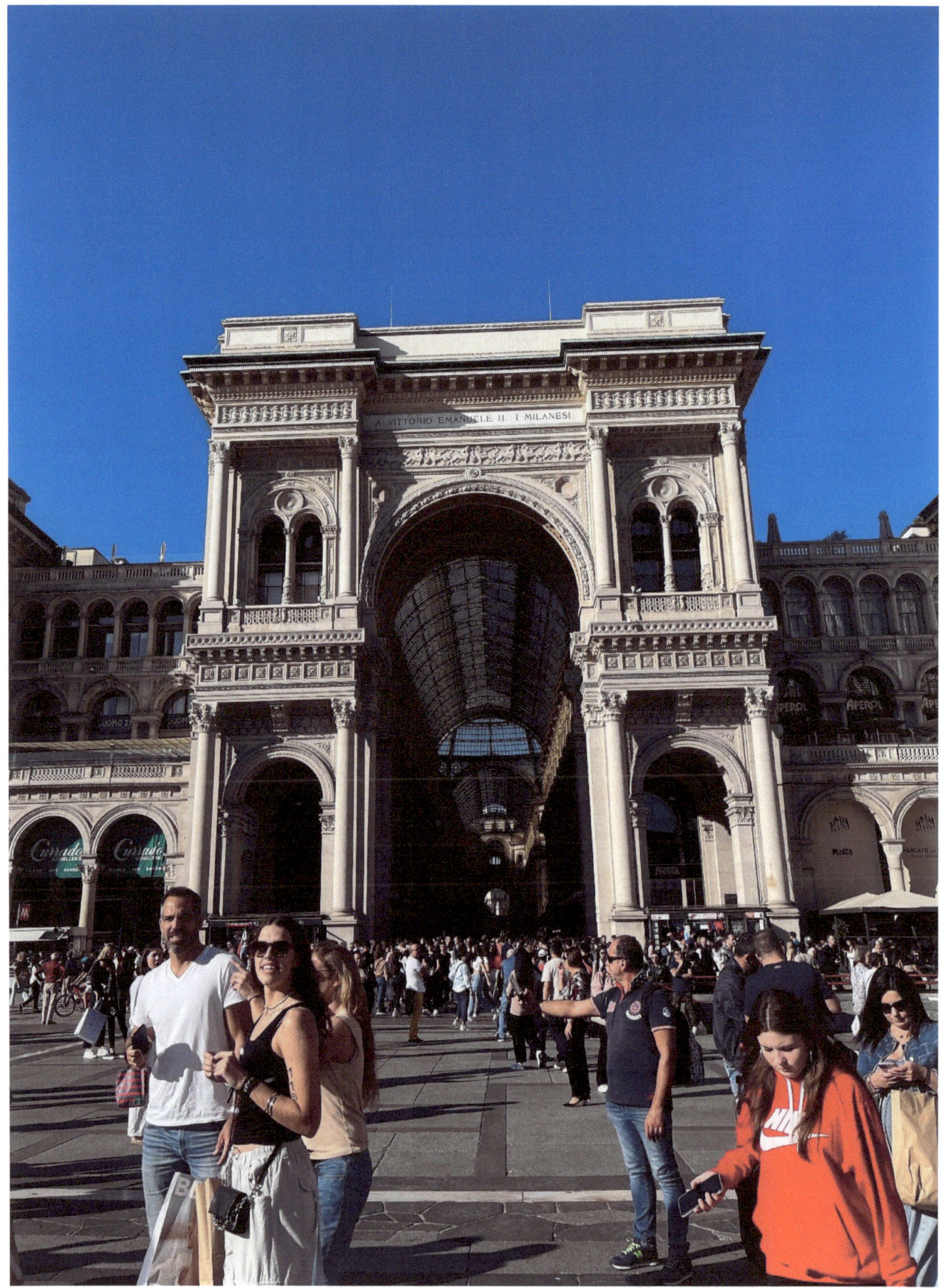

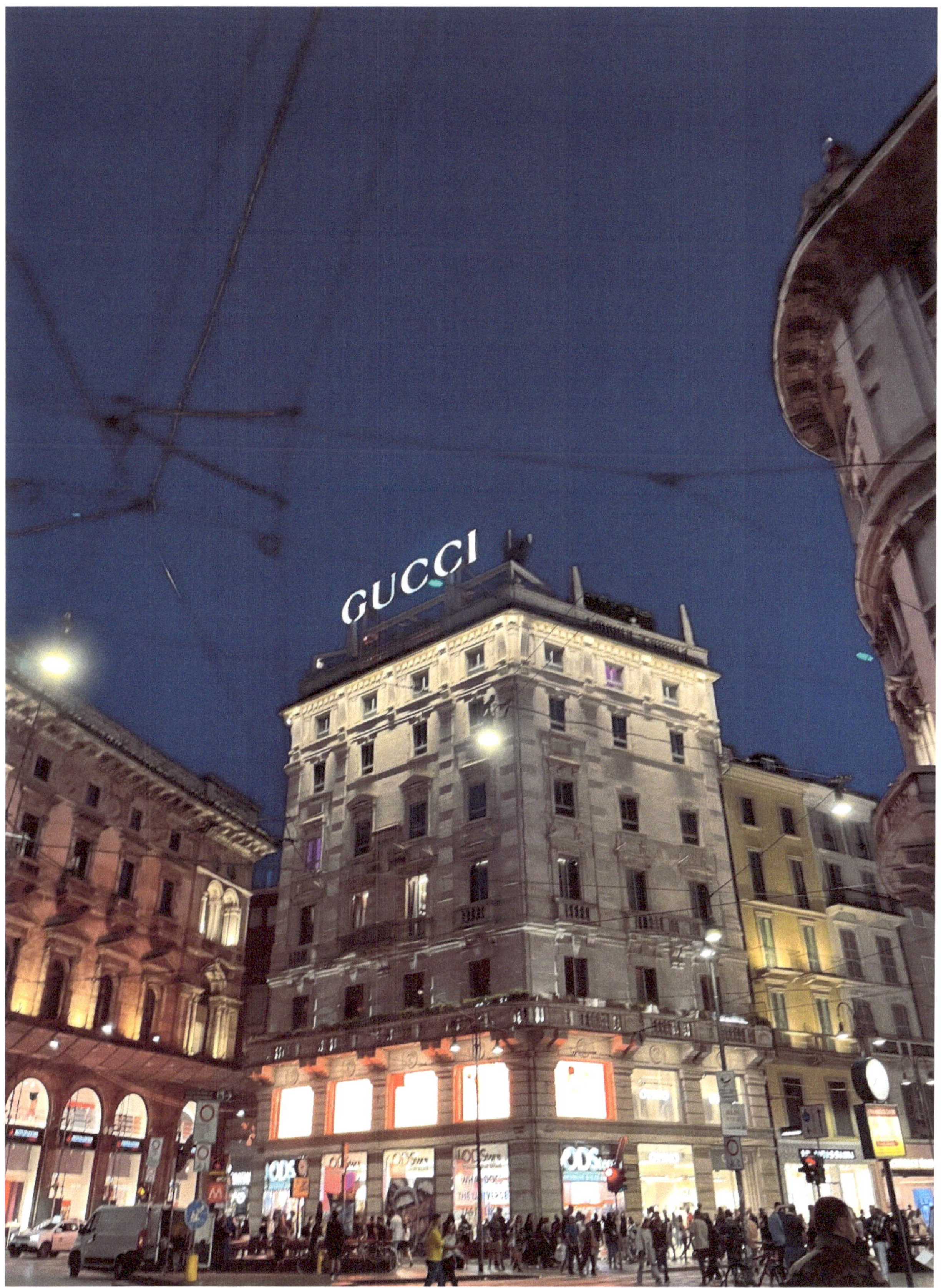
GUCCI

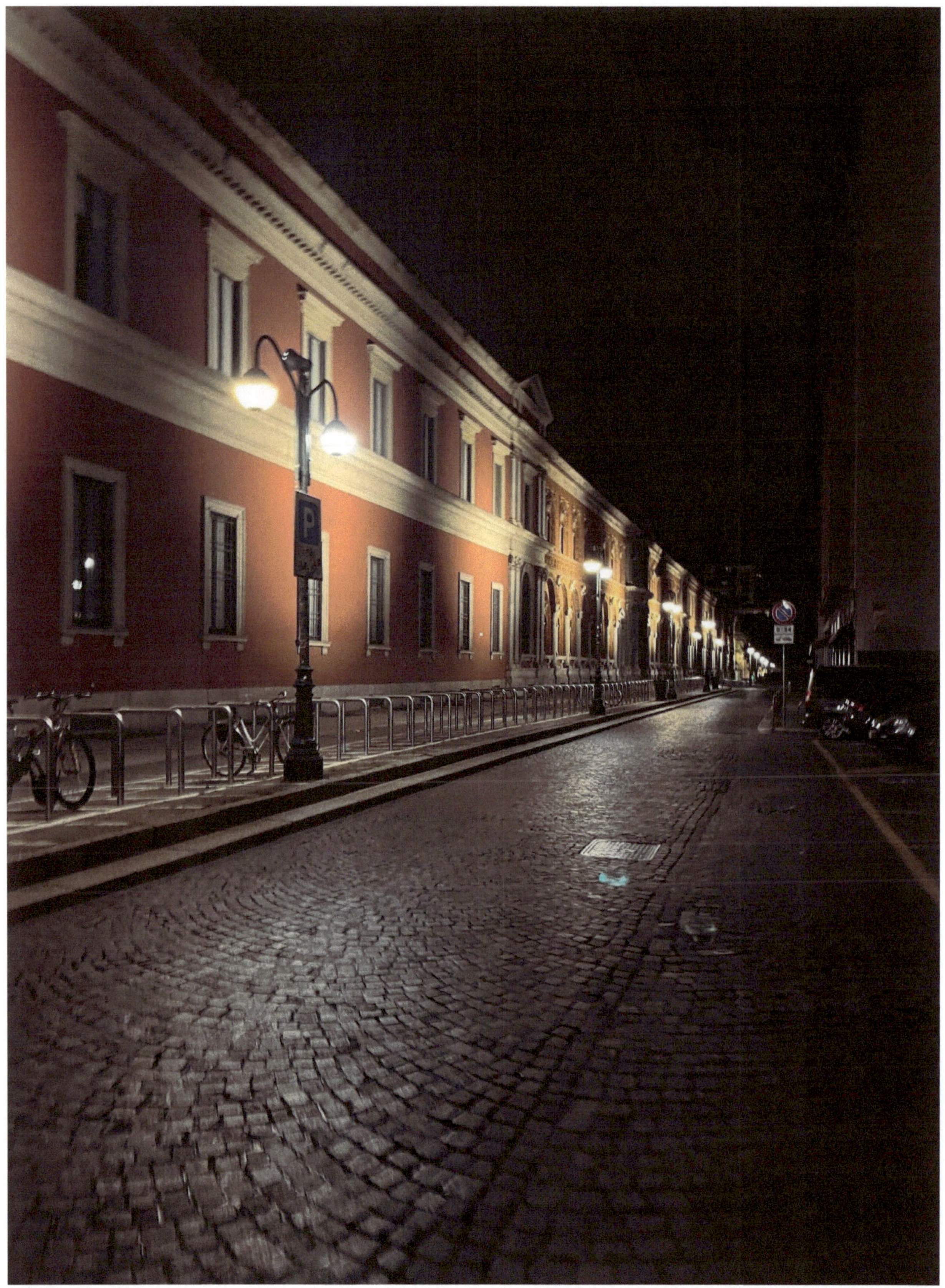

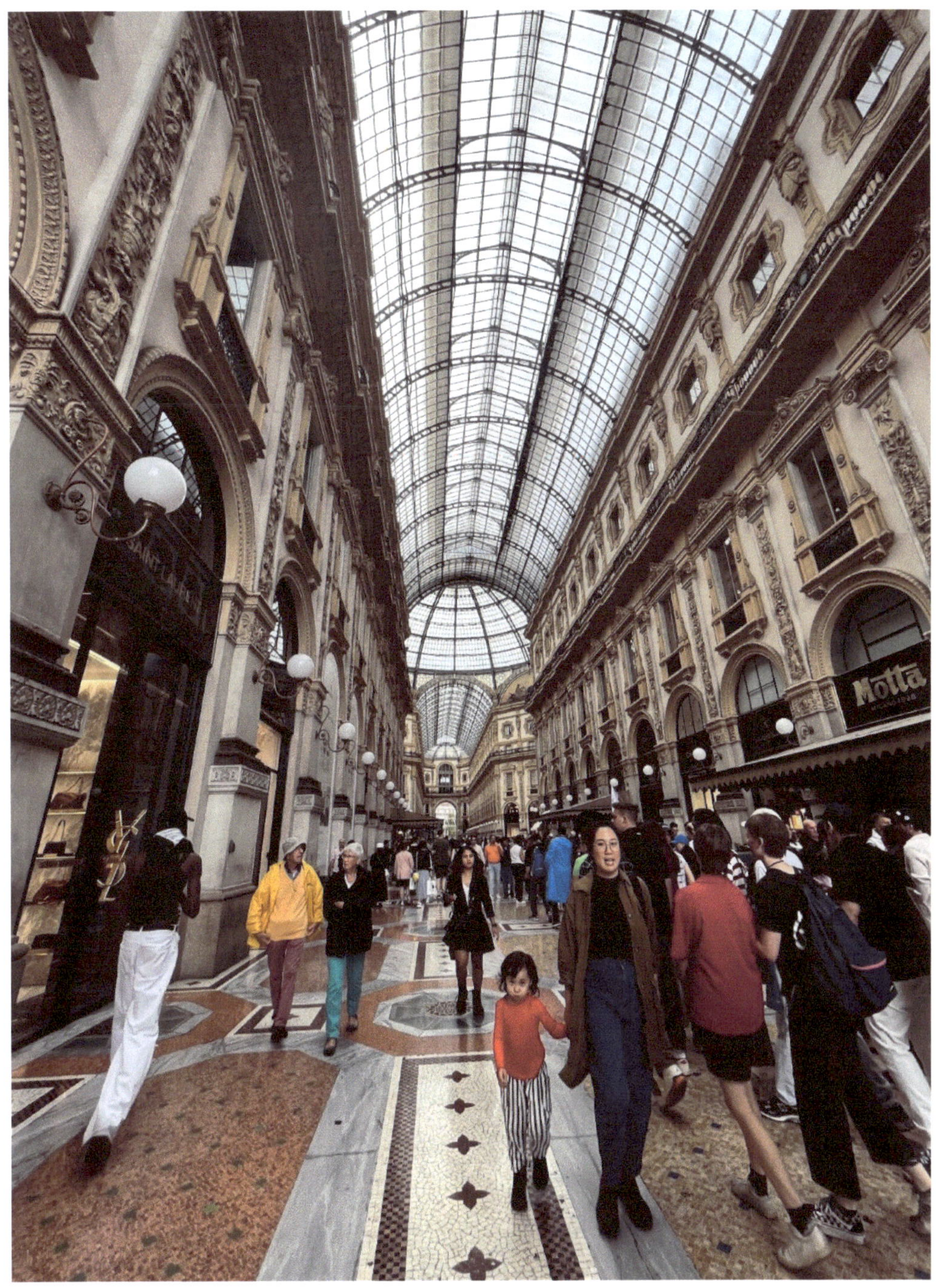

Milan, Italy is one of the most scenic locales in the world. Italy is the home of many of the world's still renowned artists including Michelangelo, Leonardo, and Raphael.

A more recent modern artist of Italy is our friend Claudio Parentela, who I interviewed about his art last year.

CLAUDIO PARENTELA

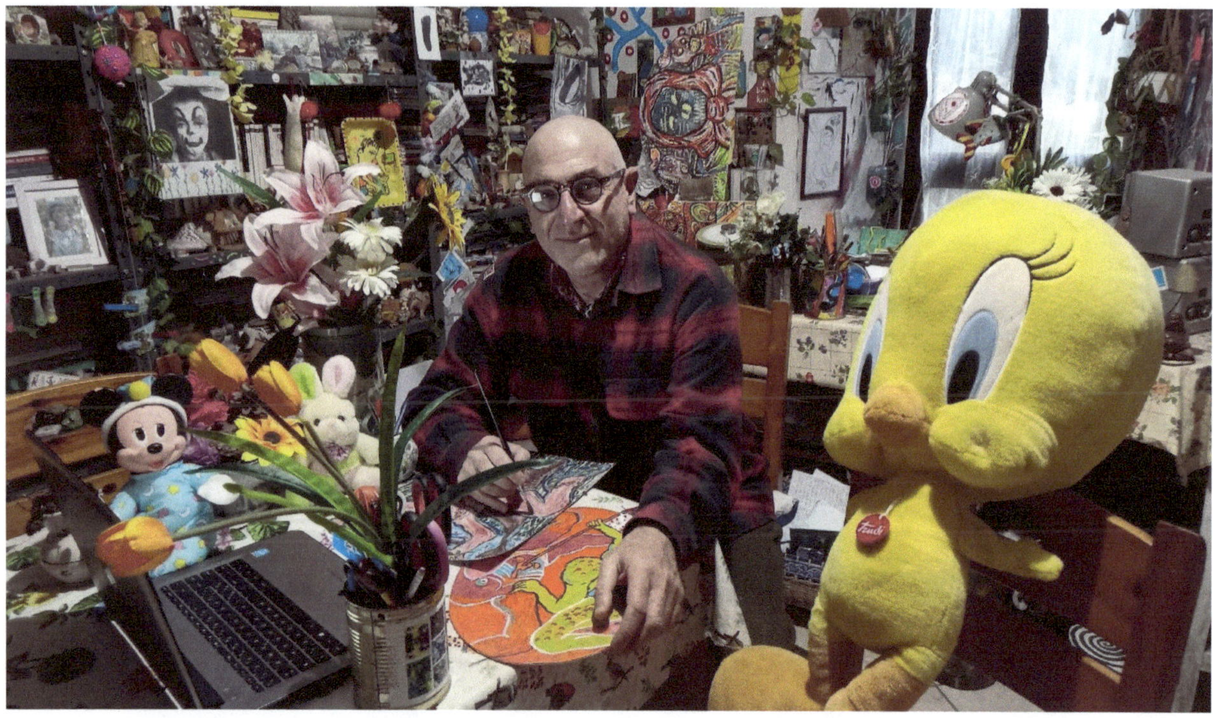

Ciao Claudio,

First tell us about your early days, and when you realized you wanted to become an Artist.

Oh ... I've always been determined about what I wanted to do in life but undecided about everything at the same time ... I've done so many different things ... then suddenly, for a variety of circumstances, I found in front of myself and what my heart really wanted .... I was 35 when I decided that I wanted to live on art, and that I wanted to breathe art all day ... for all the days of my life. I have always drawn and painted, ever since I was a child ... I remember drawing strange beings with big eyes that fought fierce and bloody battles on faraway worlds ... I have always drawn very big eyes that looked away, that looked at unexplored worlds, that looked in my soul and in the soul of the world .... today I am happy to have made this choice, because I feel free and real and faithful to what my heart was suggesting and asking for.

Were you inspired by early renaissance masters, like da Vinci, and Michelangelo Bounarroti?

Oh yes, I love the genius and perfection of both, a continuous source of inspiration for me! I love the vastness of the fields explored by Leonardo Da Vinci, his continuous and inexhaustible curiosity, the search of both for a perfection never reached, always perfectible...the patient study of a lifetime, the continuous work, the lively intelligence, the love for the experimentation, for the research, for the truth.

Wonderful, and Where did you study art?

I am proudly, anarchically, joyfully and totally a self-taught artist!

Have you been interviewed or published in America or shown in America?

Yes of course, I have been doing that beautiful "job" for many years as I told you... I have exhibited and have been published widely in America.

Where have you exhibited in Italy?

In many independent galleries.

What is your favorite subject to draw or paint?

I like to illustrate, draw, paint, photograph, the folds, the thousand folds of the human soul ... how the soul can hide in the folds of a dress, in the gesture of a hand, in a hidden smile.

Where would you like to be exhibited in the future?

But of course among the ancient stones of the Colosseum no?!

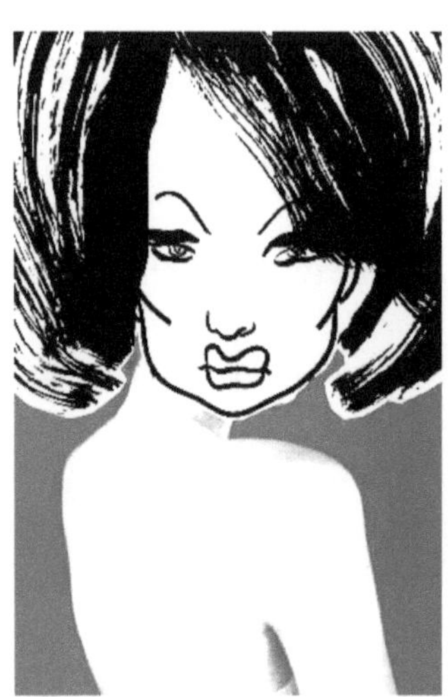

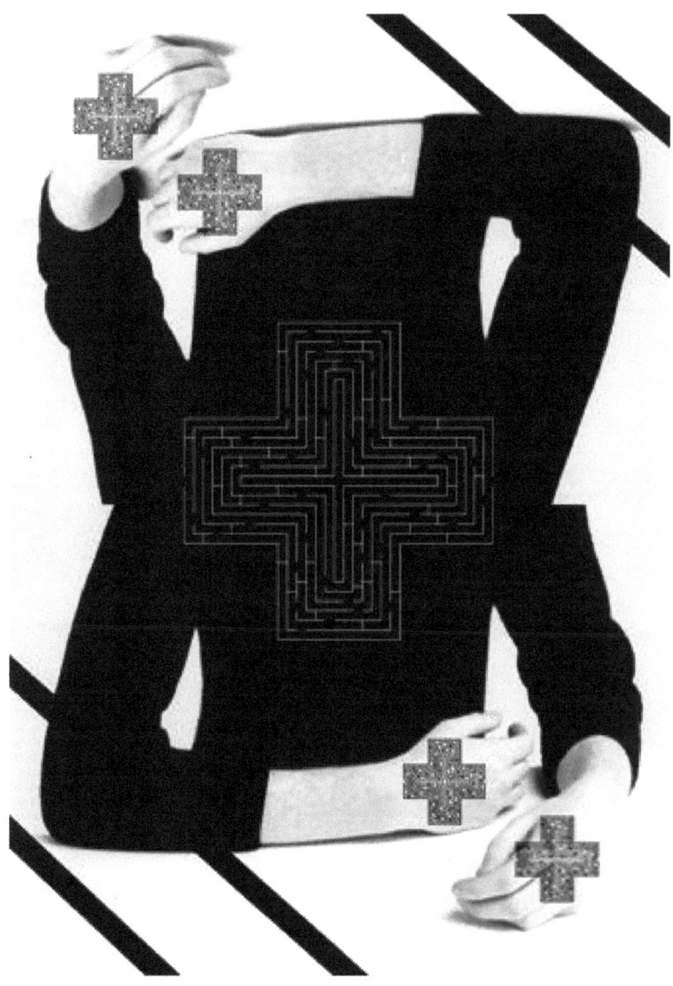

"As I see it, the art of Claudio employs a collage-based formula, one or another thing be it whatever near he will 'assemble' into a work of art.

If no ready image is at hand he will manufacture one from scratch, using his cartooning skills, and knowledge of figure illustration techniques.

A newspaper or other printed cut-out will become the backdrop of his ready-made tinted surface via printer. As Artist the necessity for recycling is necessary to voice new thoughts, in a new way, without wasting what resources, we simply annex what no longer has value and add value to what was momentarily deemed obsolete. A by-product of recycling is profit as the Artists materials are of little value to some, have been created for nearly nothing, and when sold one hundred percent profit will result.”

“The works varying in size, have a whimsical charm about them, as if to say…Don't take life too seriously!”

-EM

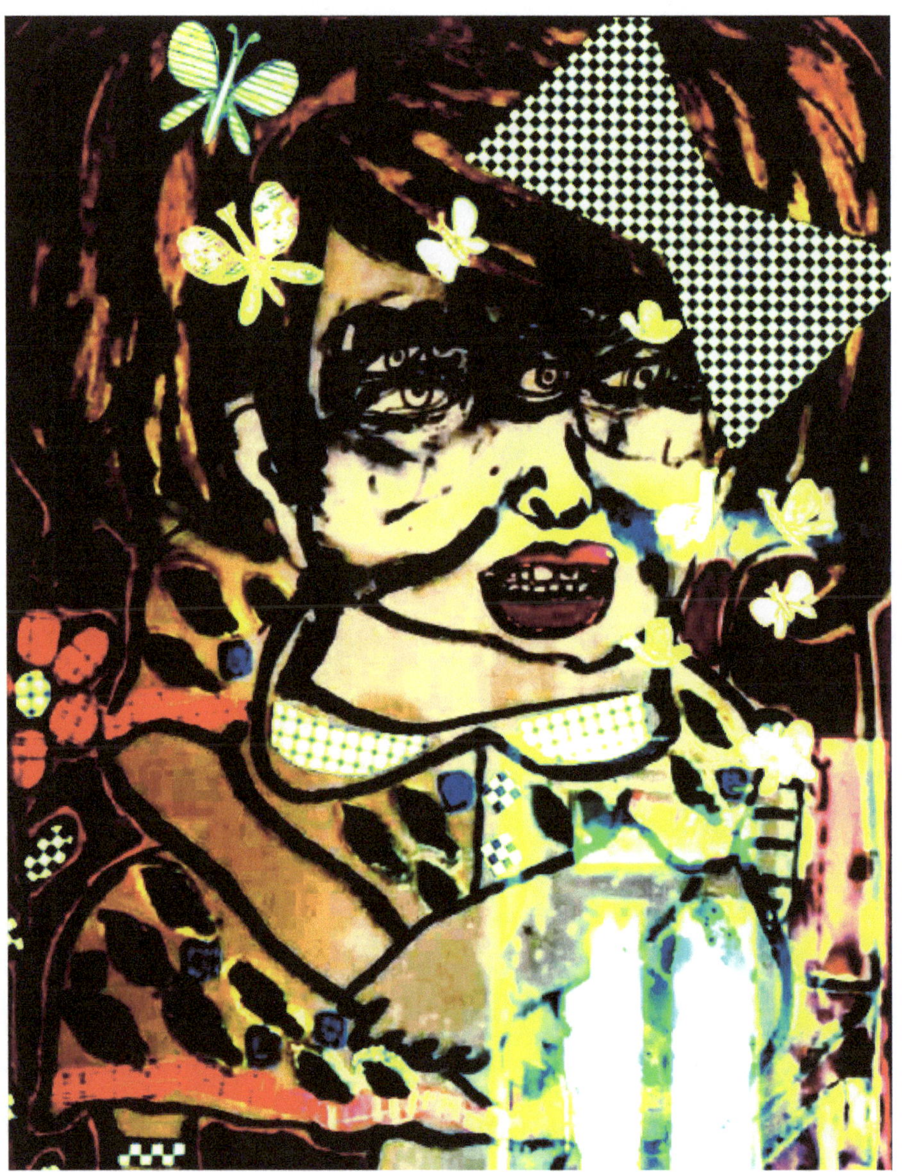

ORIGINAL PAINTINGS BY CLAUDIO PARENTELA

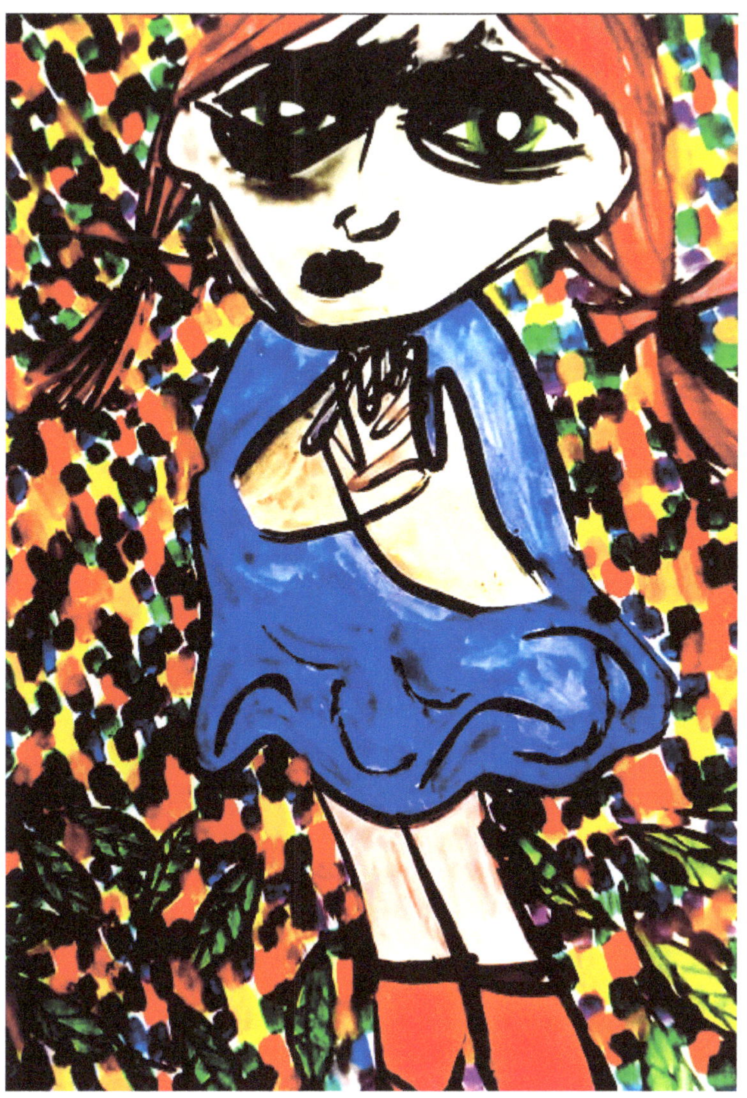

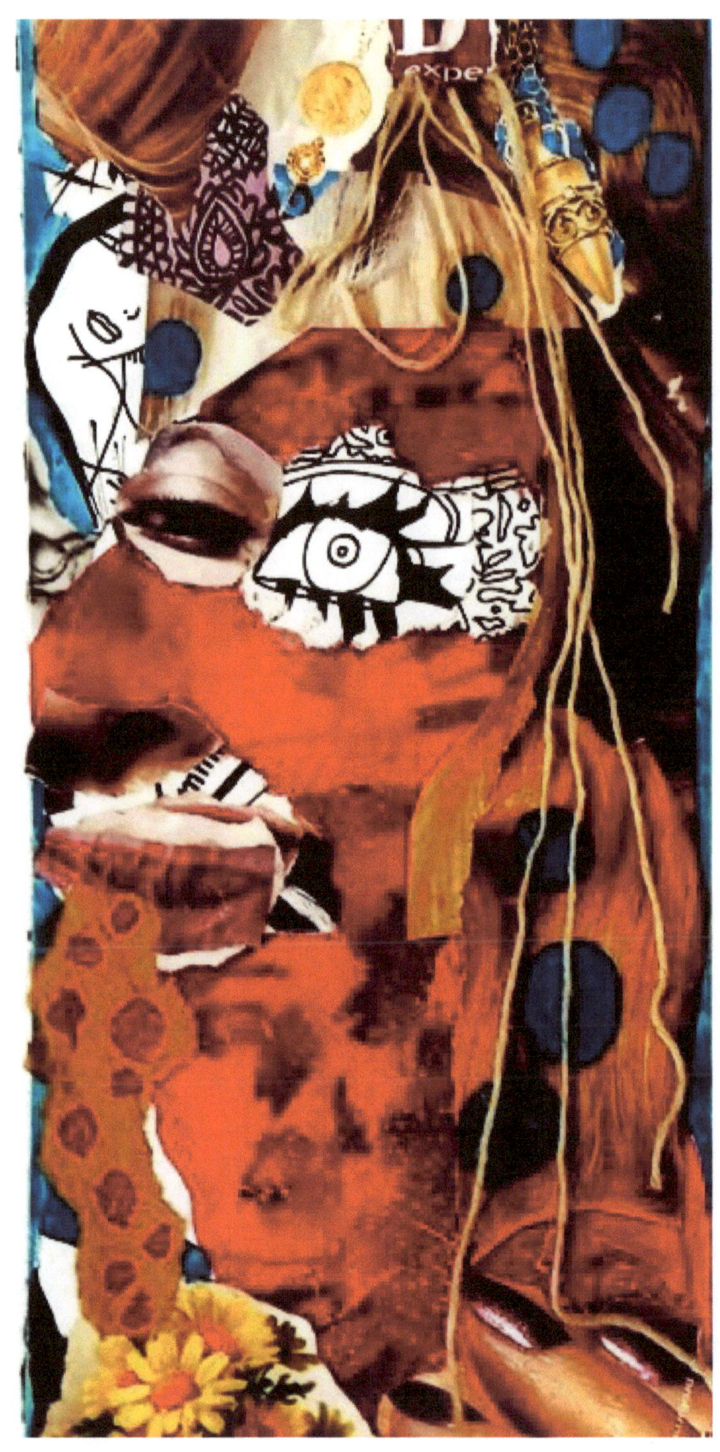

PEN & INK ON PAPER SERIES APPEAR ON THE FOLLOWING PAGES.

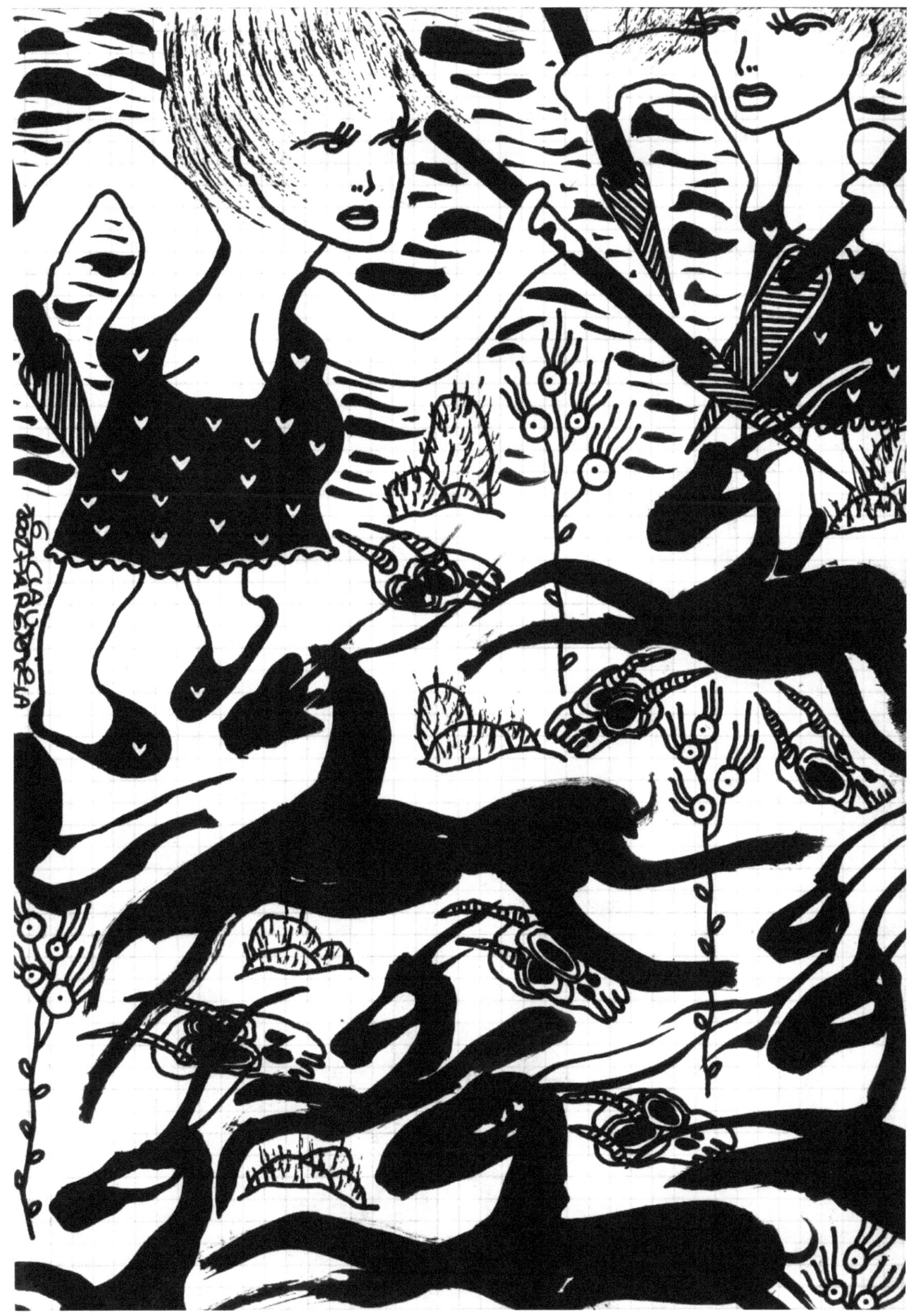

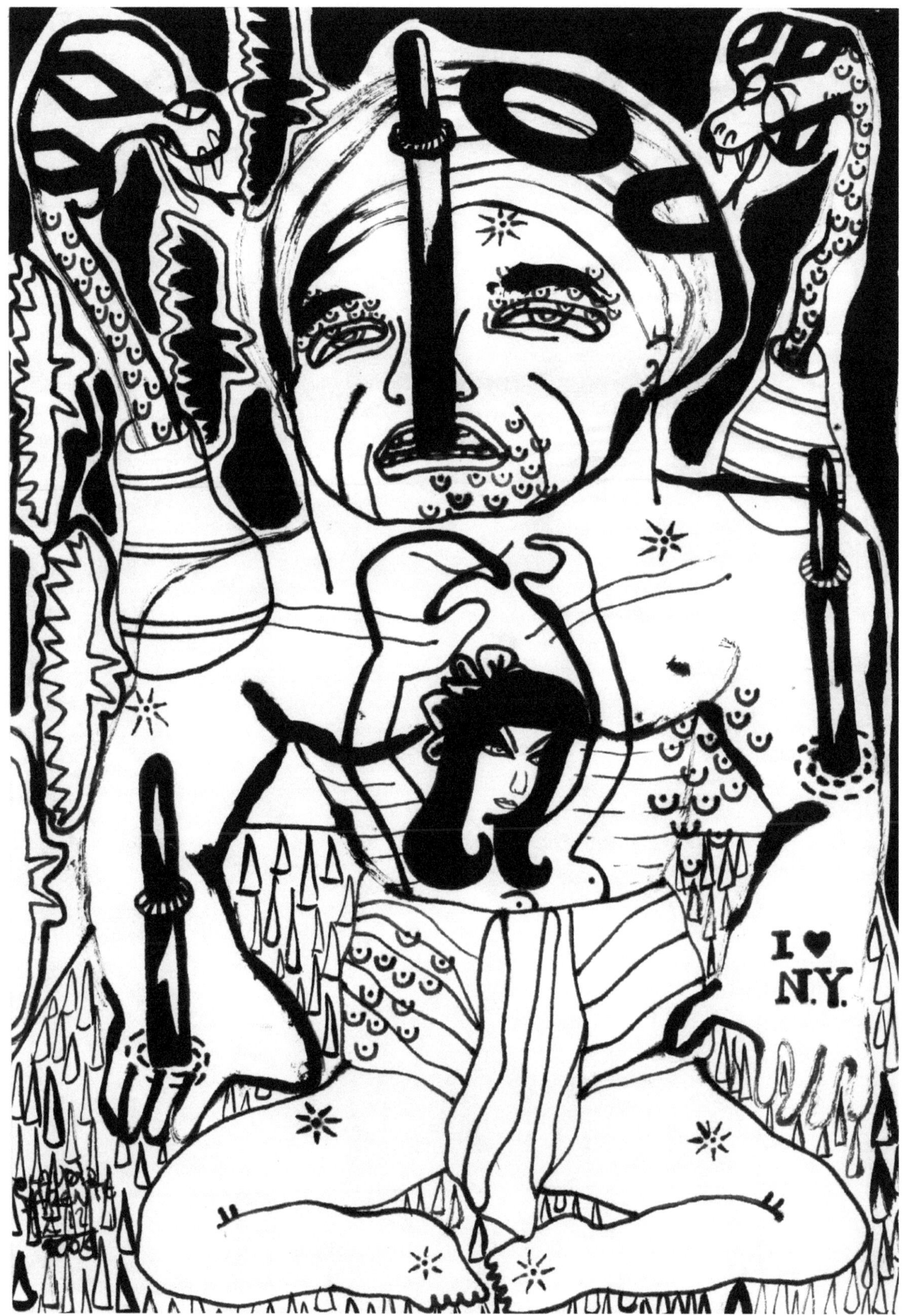
I ♥ N.Y.

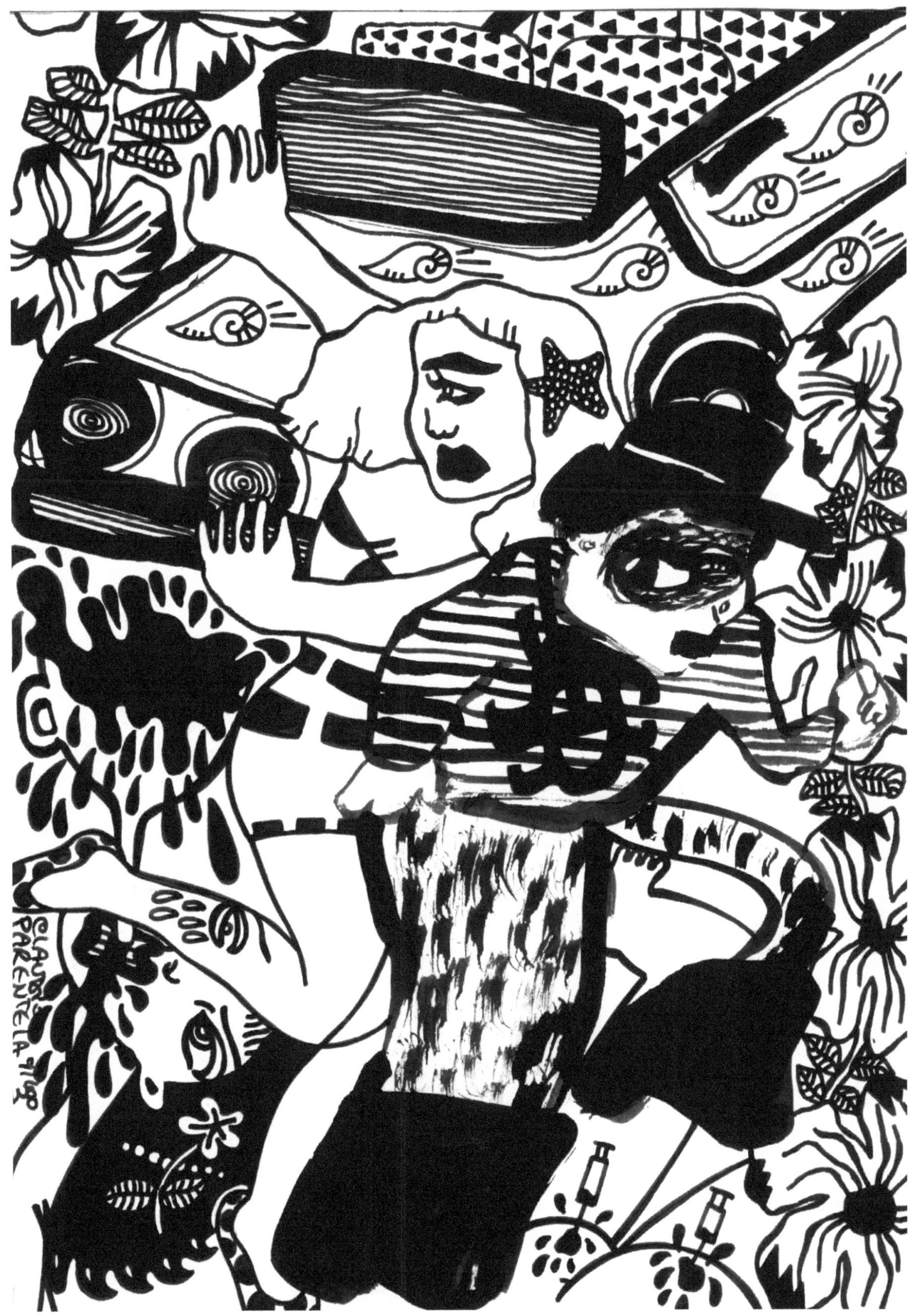

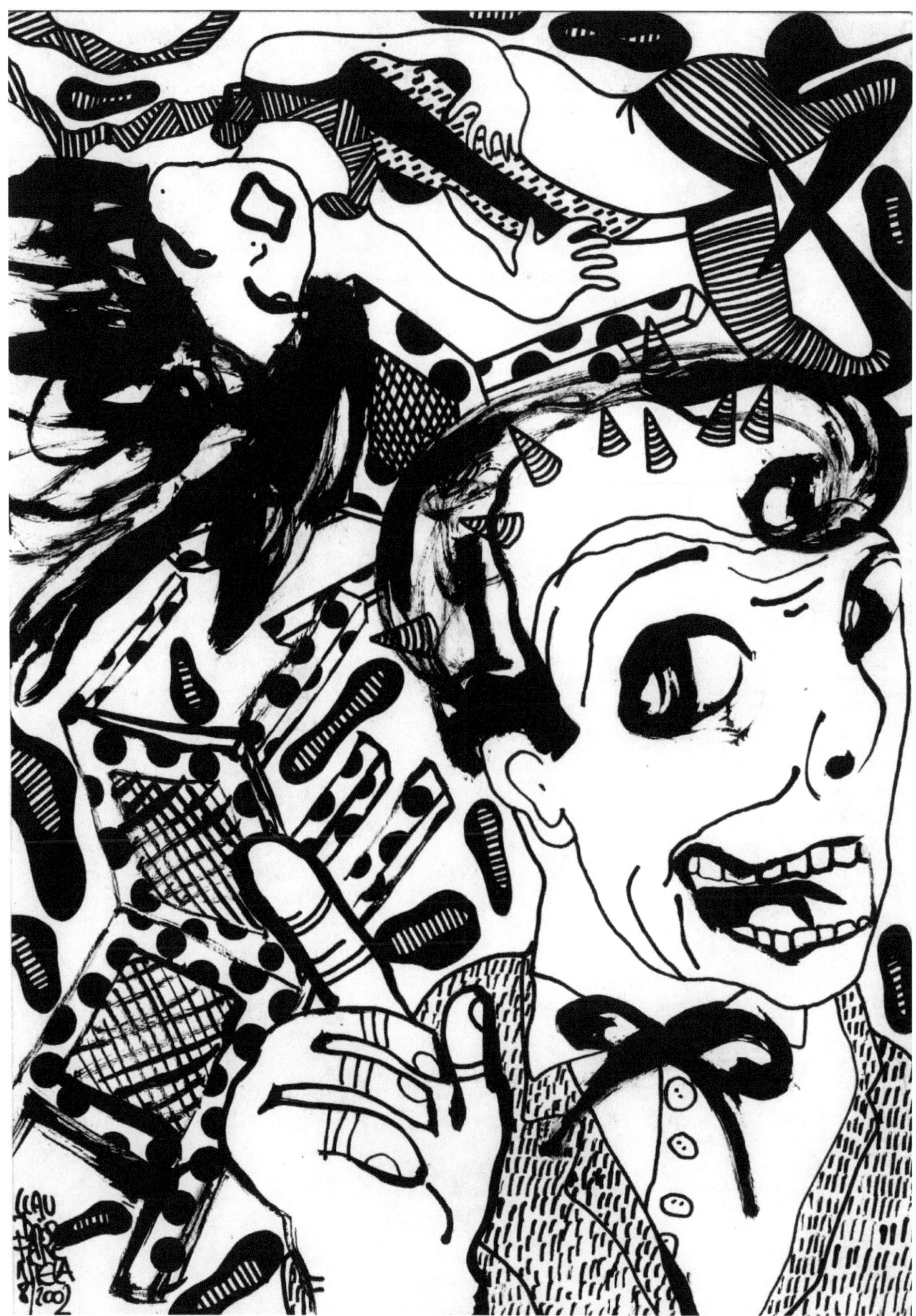